The Great Big Book Of Memes

The Definitieve Book Of Funny Memes

Introduction

Thank you for purchasing this book: The Great Big Book Of Memes.

This book covers the topic of memes, and will teach you about what a meme is, what makes a meme, common memes as well as hundreds of memes for all to enjoy.

At the completion of this book your sides will be hurting from so much laughter and you should have a good understanding of what a meme is.

Once again, thanks for downloading this book, I hope you find it to be helpful!

What Is A Meme?

If you have ever used the internet? Then you would have heard of memes but what are they?

A meme in most cases is a picture on the internet with a funny or relatable caption. They are created by people and then uploaded to the internet. Memes are then copied and spread quickly through the internet by users sharing them with their friends, family and even strangers through social media. Memes are not only pictures with captions but also can be videos and pieces of text such as text message conversations, twitter posts, Facebook posts and quotes from movies or famous people.

Memes are most commonly spread through social media. Facebook having hundreds, maybe thousands of pages dedicated to creating and sharing memes to the world.

The most common memes are quotes from movies or pictures from a movie with a caption. The caption may not be accurate to the movie, they will often vary or merge multiple movies or quotes together which is what makes them humorous.

Below is an example. The man is Mr Spock who is from Star Trek, the quote is "May the force be with you" which is from Star Wars and Dr Who isn't from either of those Sci Fi series but from his own tv show called Dr Who.

Common Types of Memes

There are many types of memes. They can involve dogs, cats, sports stars, movie stars, cartoons, games and many more.

Some of the common memes found are listed below,

1. Crazy Girlfriend

This meme is simply a picture of a girl but she looks like she is crazy and obsessive. This meme generally will her being really controlling or protective towards her boyfriend or partner.

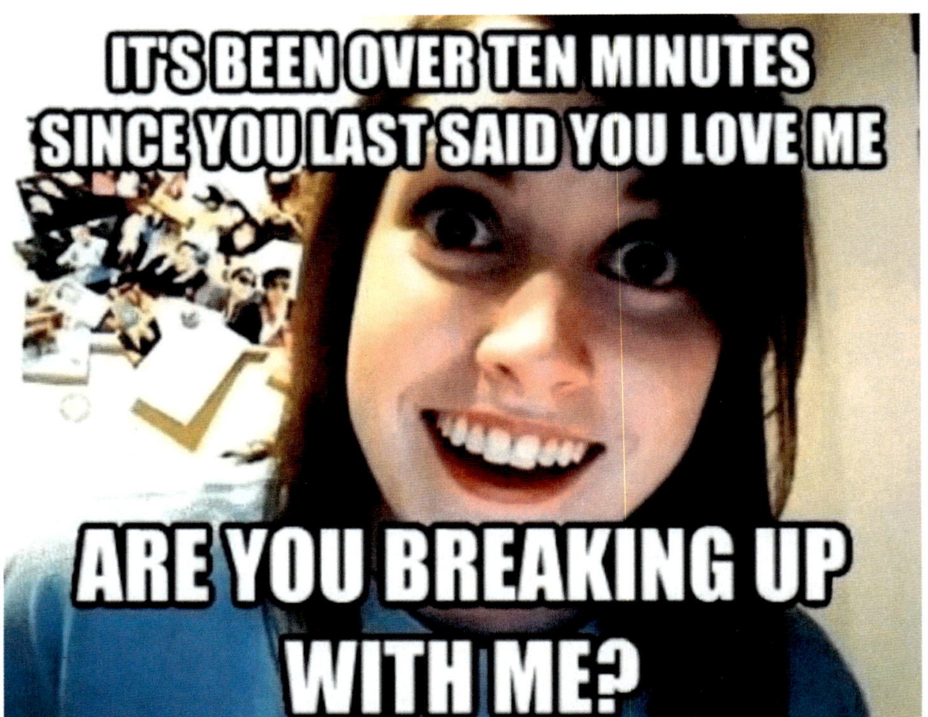

2. Stoned Guy

This one is a man who looks like he is very under the influence and doesn't know what's going on. These memes are generally him saying something so incredibly wrong or really stupid.

3. Grumpy Cat

This meme is a picture of a cat that just looks incredibly angry or grumpy. The cat always has some negative way to look at something no matter how happy or cheerful it may be.

4. Boromir "One Does Not Simply"

This meme is was created form a quote from the movie The Lord Of The Rings The Fellowship Of The Ring. The original quote was "One does not simply walk into Mordor." Theses memes generally just have a difficult task added onto the end of "One does not simply".

5. Kid Eating Sand

This meme is a picture of a boy at the beach eating some sand but the facial expression he makes with a fist full of sand makes it look like he is fist pumping. This meme is used for when you have a win or some good luck.

These are only a few of the common and more popular memes. New ones are made everyday. There are thousands of memes all different to each other.

Some people have become unexpectedly semi famous for being turned into a meme. Their fame will usually die just as quick as it grew. There are memes tailored for all different kinds of humor. You never know what could turn out to be the next big hit.

By now you should have a good idea of what a meme is and what makes a meme.

Now without further adieu, here are the memes...

when you wake up in the middle of the night to check your phone and it's on full brightness

HOW TO DO
THE PERFECT DEADLIFT
It's called "the bend and snap."

AND THEN I SAYS TO HER, I SAYS,
NO, I GOT YOUR NOSE.

LIEUTENANT DAN!
YOU GOT NEW LEGS!

YOU EITHER LOVE STAR TREK...
OR YOU'RE WRONG.

Why don't you like sand?
A: It's coarse
B: It's rough
C: It's irritating
D: It gets everywhere

MERRY CHRISTMAS
YA FILTHY ANIMAL

When you take your food out of the microwave and it burns your hand

WHAT IF I TOLD YOU
I ALREADY TOLD YOU AND
YOU DIDN'T LISTEN

SORRY I ANNOYED YOU
WITH MY LOVE

JIM CARREY
JIM DOESN'TCARREY

WHO NEEDS EXPERIENCE
WHEN YOU GOT SWAG
quickmeme.com

When the teacher is watching you during a test..

GUHHH I'M
KENDRICK LLAMA

I FEEL GOOD FROM MY HEAD
TOMATOES

If you havin hull problems,
I feel bad for you son
I got 99 problems, but a breach ain't 1

FACE YOU MAKE WHEN
KIDS ARE PLAYING NEAR YOUR CAR

PALEO BROWNIES, PALEO CUPCAKES, PALEO MUFFINS, PALEO COOKIES, PALEO FUDGE, PALEO BREAD...
PLEASE, TELL ME MORE ABOUT YOUR "HUNTER GATHERER" DIET...

when you eating an oreo and dunk it in milk but it breaks off and sinks to the bottom.

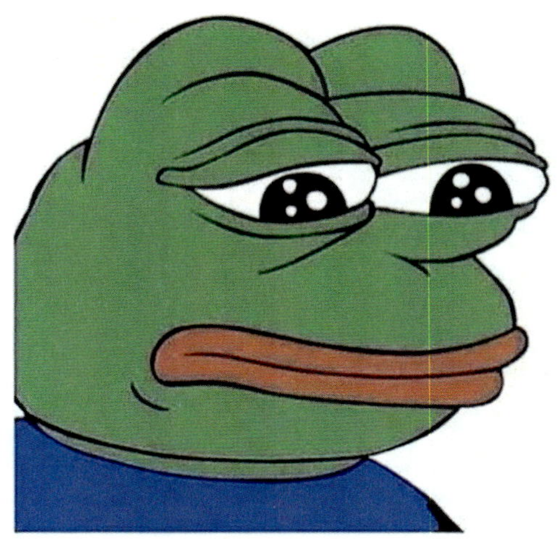

When you solve a maths problem 3 times

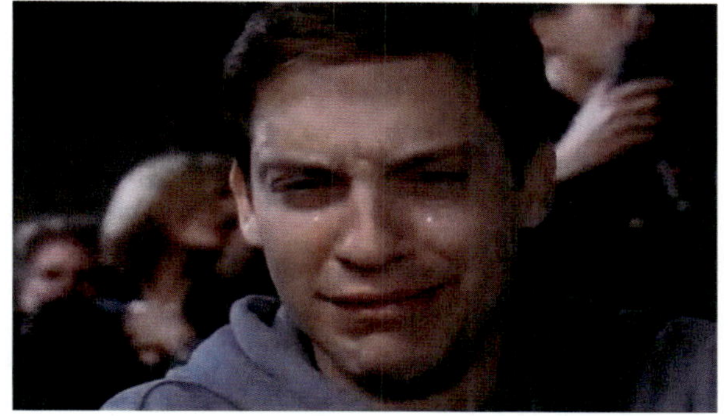

and get different answer each time

LOVE IS IN THE AIR?
GET OUT THE GAS MASK

i don't always leave my boyfriend alone
but when i do
there is a small recording device under his sleeve

I'M ON A SEAFOOD DIET
I SEE FOOD AND I EAT IT.

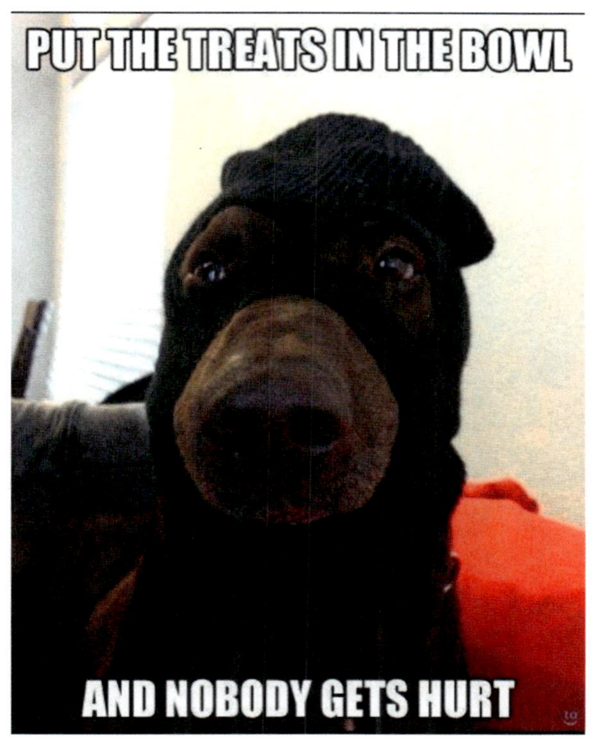
PUT THE TREATS IN THE BOWL
AND NOBODY GETS HURT

CHUCK NORRIS BUILT
THE HOSPITAL
THAT HE WAS BORN IN

I WORSHIP THE
OLD GODS
YOU'VE PROBABLY
NEVER HEARD OF THEM

MY FACE
When someone tells me
they are not into Halloween

WHEN YOU ALREADY
STARTED EATING
AND SOMEONE SAYS
"LETS PRAY"

STILL MORE EXPRESSIONS
THAN KRISTEN STEWART

WORLD'S BEST
ARCHEOLOGIST
DESTROYS EVERY ANCIENT
TEMPLE HE ENTERS

YEA, WELL...
THAT'S LIKE...
YOUR OPINION MAN!

When people ask when I want to eat
Every day. All day. Anywhere. Anytime.

Robber: Give me all you got on you.

Drake: Here...take my wallet....she already stole my heart....

VLADISLAV
BABY DON'T HURT ME,
DON'T HURT ME, NO MORE

SO THEN IM SIAD "NO,
THIS LITTLE PIGGYS GOING TO THE BAR
imgflip.com

ONE DOES NOT SIMPLY
WALK INTO MORDOR
You underestimate my power

A BOOK FELL ON MY HEAD
I CAN ONLY BLAME MY SHELF

When someone is about to remind the teacher about the homework

After you tell somebody "bless you" twice and they keep sneezing

I DON'T ALWAYS SURF THE INTERNET
BUT WHEN I DO
EYEBROWS

IF YOU SAY YOUR EXES NAME 3 TIMES IN THE MIRROR
DRAKE APPEARS AND CRIES WITH YOU.

HAPPY FRIDAY!
WAIT, SORRY, IT'S MONDAY

THAT MOMENT WHEN YOU
BEAT THE CANDY CRUSH LEVEL YOU'VE BEEN STUCK ON FOREVER

When he's testing the fuck outta you and your crazy bitch side bout to shine bright like a diamond

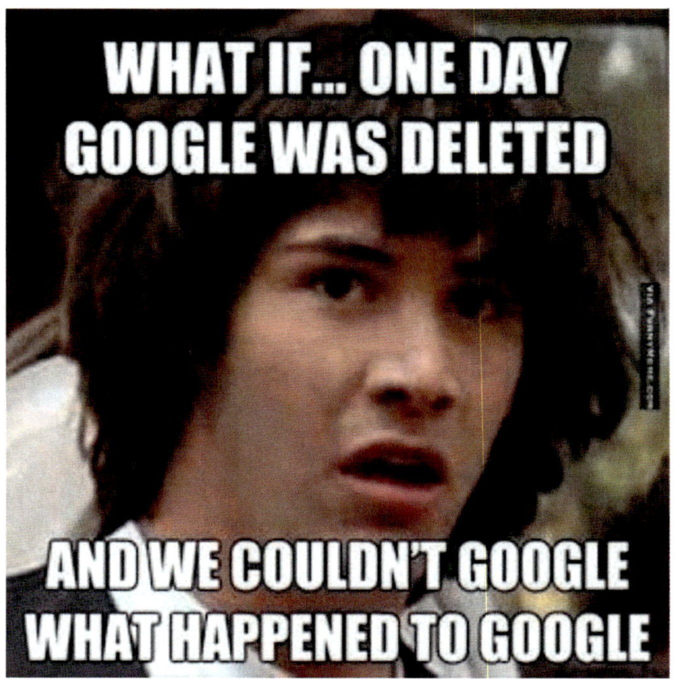

You're a man
Did you just
assume my gender?

TELETUBBIES ARE
TERRIFYING
IN BLACK AND WHITE

I STILL
HAVE NO IDEA WHAT I'M DOING

THEN THAT MILEY GIRL GOT
UP THERE AND TWERKED
WITHOUT ANY BUT-TOCKS

Roses are red,
Harambe's in heaven...

Unquestionable proof that Bush did 9/11

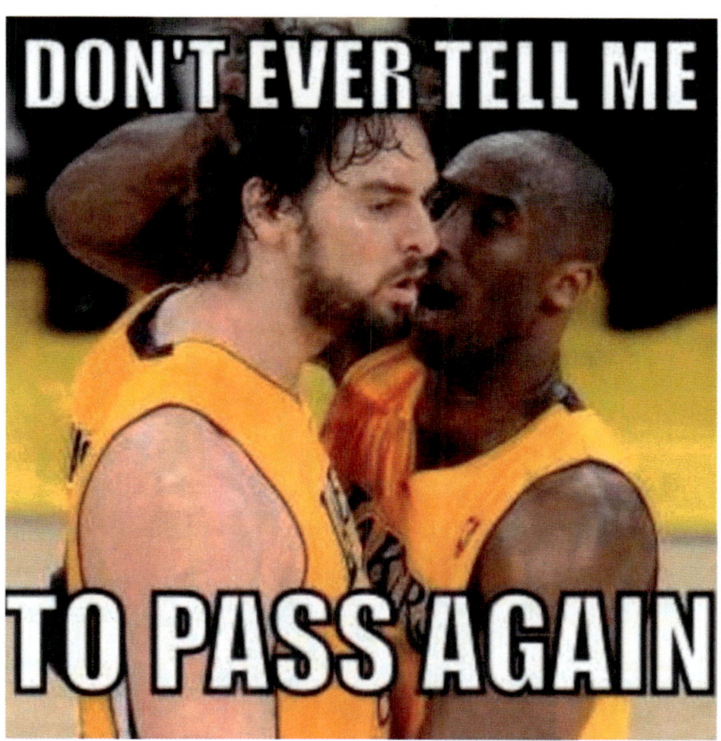

BEST MATHEMATICIANS

HAHAHA
GREAT POST!

WELL MEME'D
MY FRIEND!

When I go back and read that text I sent him of me spazzing the fuck out and say to myself "I'm crazy" lmao

MOM SAYS: ALCOHOL IS YOUR ENEMY.
JESUS SAYS: LOVE YOUR ENEMY. CASE CLOSED.

What people think Boromir looks like when he says
"One does not simply"

What he really looks like.

SO WE MEET AGAIN.
FOR THE LOVE OF GOD, BATMAN..
I'M NOT THE JOKER !

EXCUSE ME
JUST FOR A MOMENT

MY BED TIME IS 7:00
BUT I GO TO BED AT
7:05
THUG LIFE

THE FIRST DAY OF
SCHOOL
AND YOU SEE SOMEONE YOU DON'T
LIKE WHO IS NOW IN YOUR CLASS

I DON'T ALWAYS SAY SOMETHING STUPID
BUT WHEN I DO, I KEEP TALKING TO MAKE IT WORSE

DON'T THROW THAT BALL TO ME
BULLS
23
I JUST GOT MY NAILS DID

I COULD
SPATEN
SPATEN
GOPHER A BEER

BACK IN MY DAY
WE DIDN'T HAVE BACK
IN MY DAY MEMES

I BELIEVE THIS CAT IS
INBRED

LITTLE OLD LADIES IN WHEELCHAIRS
WITH BLANKETS OVER THEIR LEGS,
YOU AREN'T FOOLING ME...
RETIRED
MERMAIDS.

How do people starve like just eat something bruh lol

When u promised to work out, do laundry, clean and go to bed early, but then get home from work and sit there like this for 4 hours

When you see your bed after a long day

Mom: You keep failing all your tests.
Son: Mom, the only test you ever passed was your pregnancy test.

Choose your fighter

When your nose is stuffed and you just sit there and think about the time when it wasn't stuffed and how you took breathing freely for granted

Friend: shes so hot

Me: shes 14

Friend: age is just a number

Me: you know what else is just a number?

Friend: what?

Me:

Lady: who is the worlds cutest lamp?

Cat: who is the worlds loneliest alcoholic?

Lady: wow

Cat: yeah fucking hurts doesn't it?

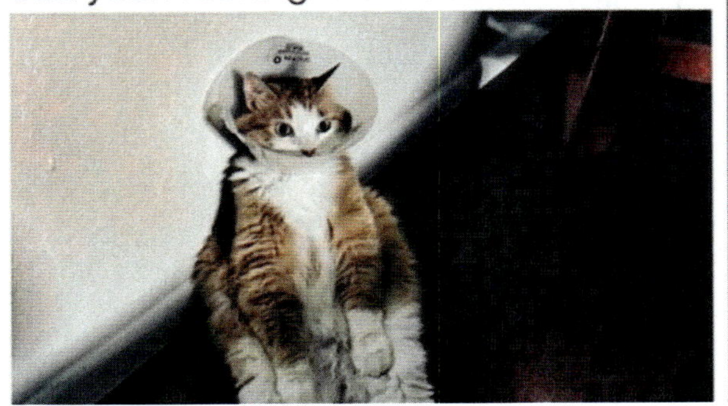

SCIENTIST: Let's name this spider Long Legs, for its long legs

SCIENTIST 2: Hmm not kinky enough

When the teacher randomly calls on you when you're spacing out

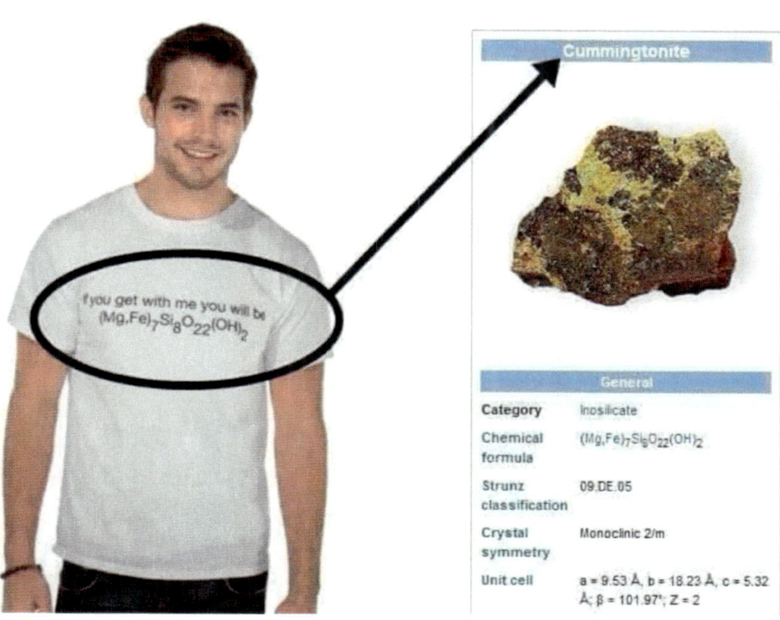

just do it 🎷

Did you just use a saxophone as a Nike icon

when you're chill but people at the party are hyper af and start screaming at you

When you check your phone in the middle of the night, but forget to turn the brightness down

when your friend forgets to give you a blanket

They always ask "who's a good boy"
never "hows the good boy"

do u ever just like flex your foot wrong and it cramps and you're just like

this is it

this is how it ends

Who ordered the shredded cheese?

Who Would Win

The Strongest Bone in The Body | One Silver Boi

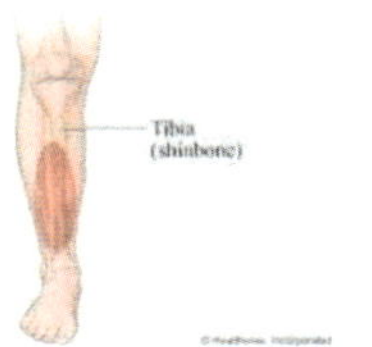

when you trying to watch netflix and she pulls a titty out

When you watch rick and morty

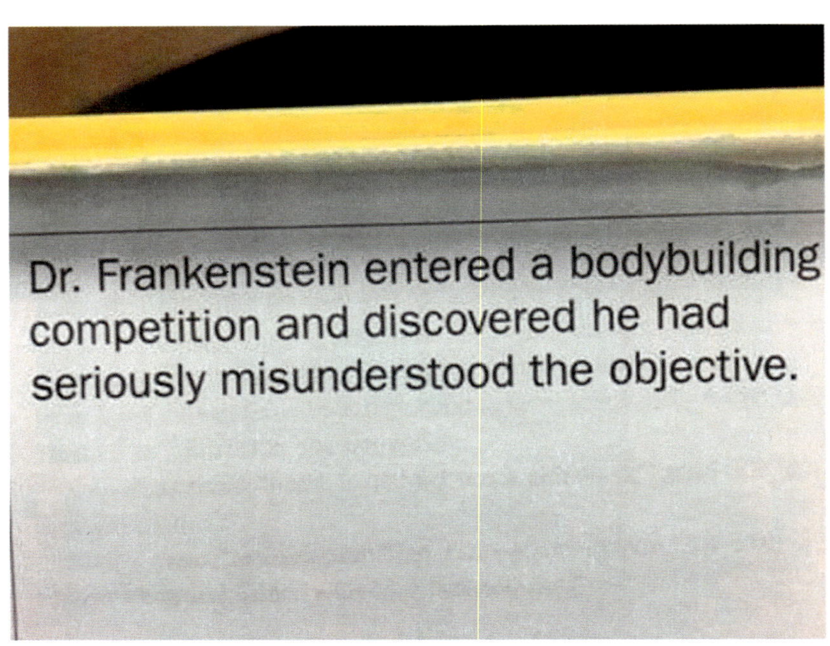

When someone opens the door to my room

you heard of Panic! At The Disco, now get ready for

You must be at least 6'2", workout, have a nice car, have strong shoulders, have a career, and a beard.

HER:

Friend: Do you want the rest of my-

Me:

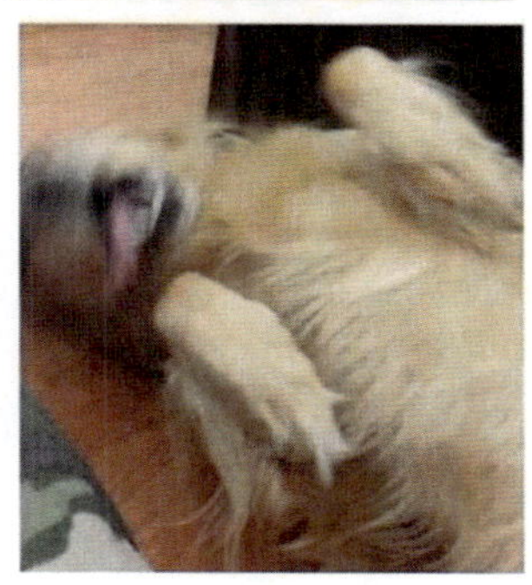

when you try to eat a light dinner because you need to save room for all the ass you're going to eat later

When you watching Chopped and a chef decides to make a vinaigrette with less than a minute left

When the wknd is over and u have to say goodbye to your real self for a few days

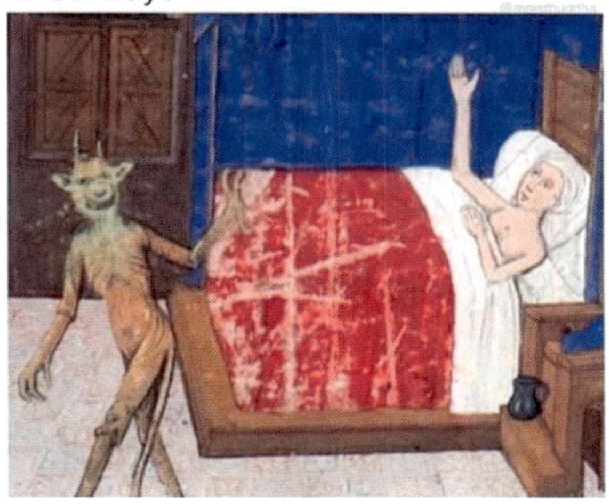

How I sleep knowing that I have a big day tomorrow and need as much rest as possible

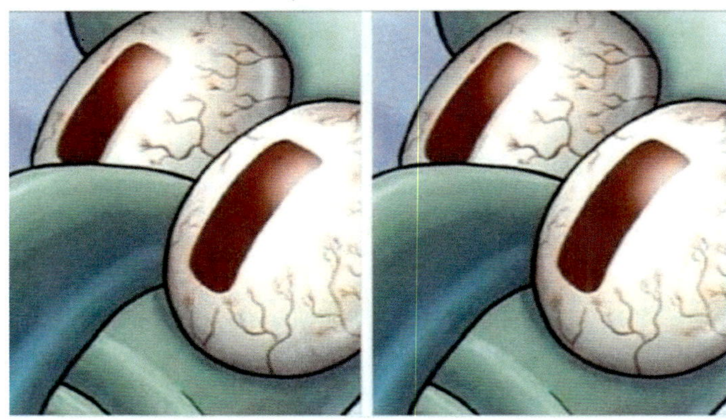

What's the time, Einstein?

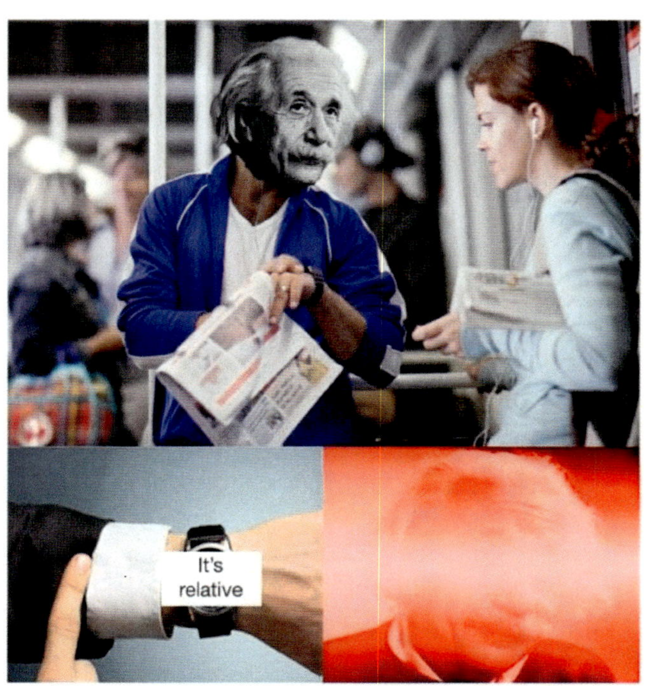

Job Interviewer: so how flexible can your hours be?

Me:

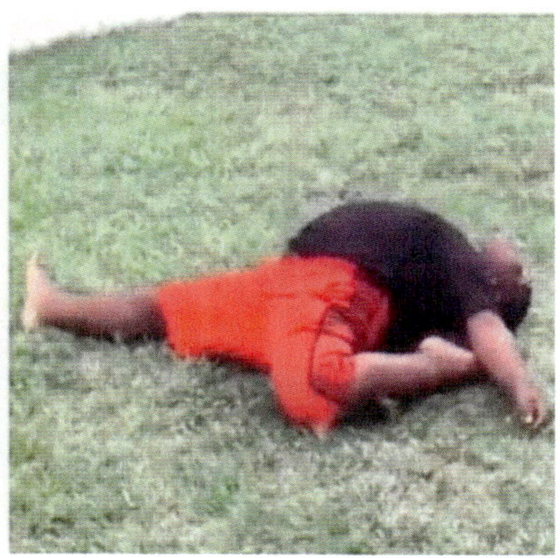

When your teacher is telling her boring ass life story,but you need her to round your 58 to a 85

She was born to be an author

Who would win?

Massively popular English language honed and perfected 1400 years	Some guy that doesn't feel hot whilst wearing a jacket

I hate when people just leave shopping carts in the middle of the aisle

at a job interview
Boss: What's ur biggest accomplishment?
Me:

CAN WE TAKE A SECOND TO APPRECIATE HOW MUCH THIS CHAIR LOOKS LIKE DUSTIN FROM STRANGER THINGS

boy: why is the food cold and bland?

dad: because your mother put her heart and soul into it

When you have to hold down the power button to turn off a device

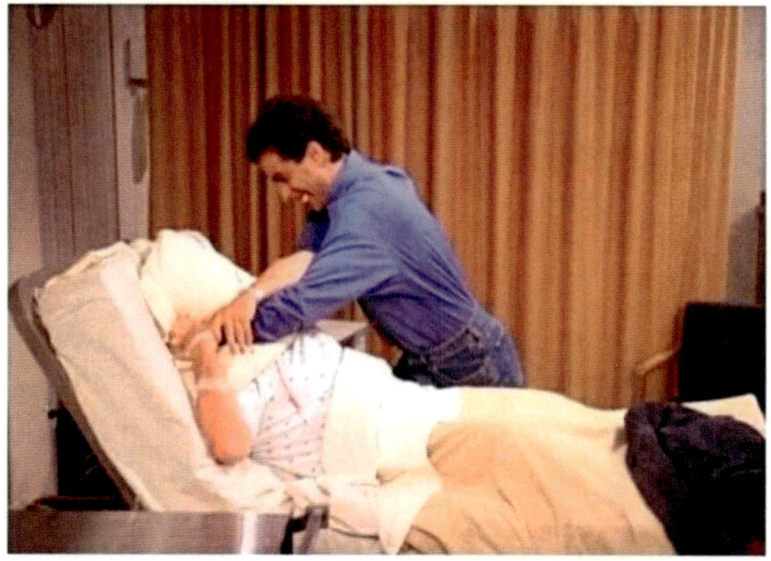

No lighter but we got science

i wanna get WASTED

W ake up early
A nticipate a productive day
S tay hydrated
T ake a multivitamin
E xercise
D ont stay up too late

10:20 AM - 23 Jul 2017

when you are sitting on your flight playing csgo and your headphones disconnect as the game loudly announces "Bomb has been planted"

when someone asks why im single

Pro tip: If you're tired of boiling water when you make pasta, just boil a few gallons at the beginning of the week and freeze it for later.

Hey kid wanna

study at Harvard **with us**

A very rare photograph of Michael Jackson performing without his glove

When your cat knows you're vegan.

UPDATE. EA announces plans for next gen controller.

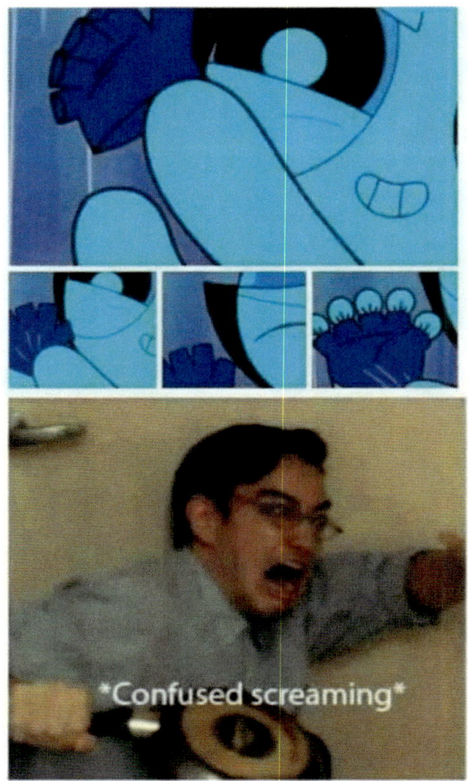

When someone comes over unannounced and catches you playing all 4 players in a game of monopoly

'What do we call this'
Now Elon, this is what we call walking.
'And humans enjoy this?'
Yes Elon. Yes they do.

"Listen dude, sarcasm will get you nowhere in life"

"Well it got me to the Sarcasm World Championships in Peru back in 98"

"Really?"

"No"

Me: what's a good show to watch on netfli...

Person 3.2 miles away: HAVE YOU SEEN STRANGER THINGS

The only thing stranger than Stranger Things is @SeanAstin 's 2005 wardrobe

Sean Astin @SeanAstin · 1d

It's called fashion sweetie look it up

270 571 6,270

me carrying all this love but no one to give it to

When I see a teacher make this face taking attendance, I know its my name.

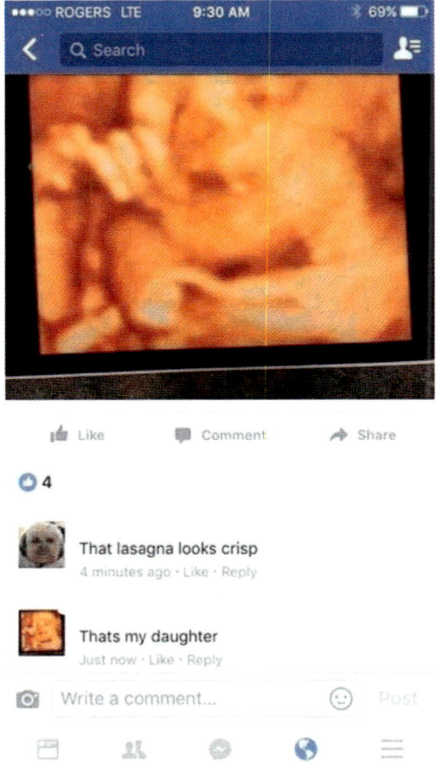

70% of single girls

Me: *Pours heart and soul into a text*
Her:

he is always watching

Me: Help, this man is dying. Does anyone know what I can do?

Stranger things fan: you should start watching, it's a reaaallyy good show

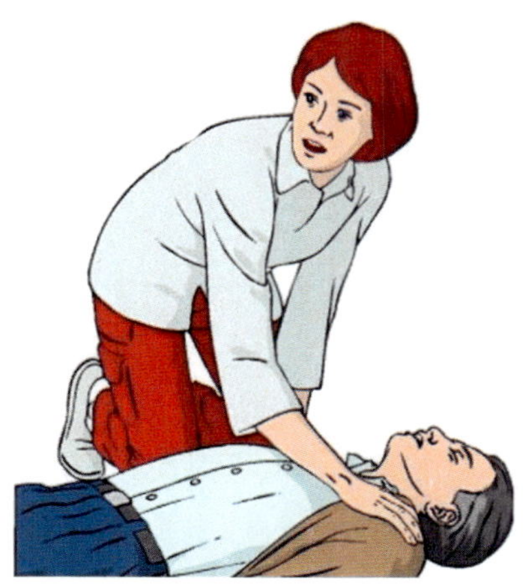

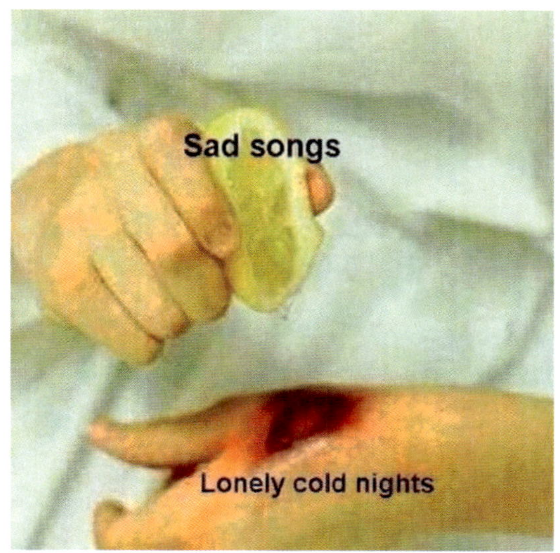

Found a brand new way to get your snacks into a movie

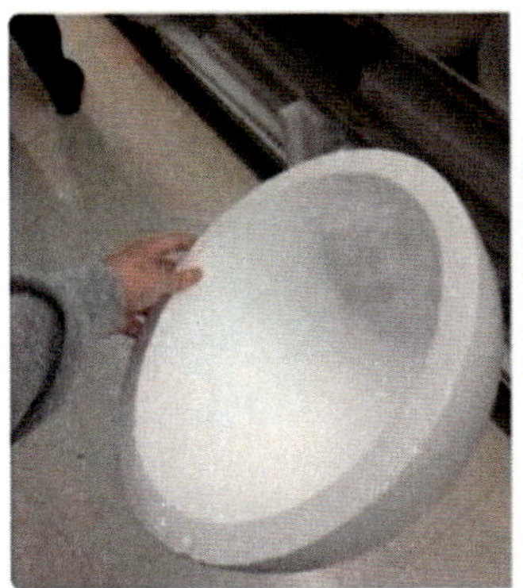

Finally we're being taught something that we can all relate to!

When your WiFi is down for ten minutes

Cop: ur car smells like marijuana

Me: whoever smelt it dealt it

Cop: gosh dangit

Me: ur under arrest

When your friends invite you to go out with them, you know you ain't going, but you act interested anyway

Today 9:26 PM

1-10: how much do you hate me?

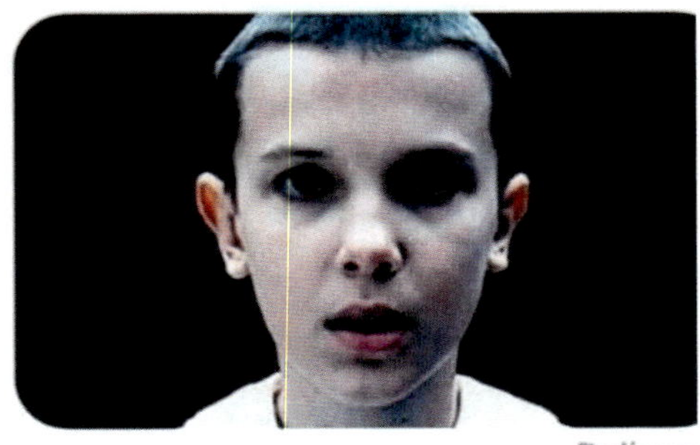

Deliver

Ok

Got it

After a year of telling my friend he looks like Bob Ross, he finally sends me this photo

When you spend most of your time looking at memes instead of getting shit done

when he brings you food>>> 😍

My anxiety watching me try to make small talk with someone I just met

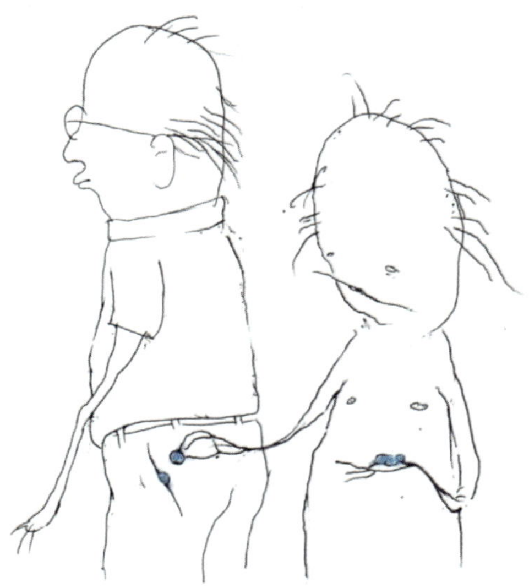

sneak a few blueberries into a stranger's pocket so they can have a little snack later.

When youtube gives you an unskippable ad

Ultra rare picture of a vegan being born

WHO WOULD WIN?

A whole institution designed to teach and train young humans in various fields

Cuddly boi

Flipper is the latest Hollywood celebrity accused of sexual assault

People: are you ok?

Me: yea

Me to me: don't study that topic it won't come up in the exam
Reads first question

When you leave ur dog at ur grandma's house for a few days

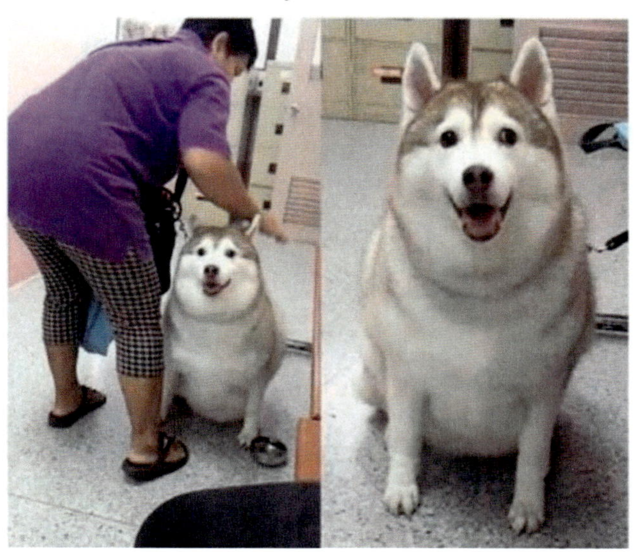

When you are at Ikea and pronounce something right

Approaching the end of this semester like

that mini heart attack when you can't feel these in your pocket

When you invite a girl over to watch star wars, and she starts taking her clothes off

Bond: My watch says u r not a VIRGIN.

Girl: But I'm still a VIRGIN.

Bond: My watch is 20 mins fast.

Your girlfriend got pregnant, you never slept with her. She says She's a virgin. When the baby is born, three guys come out of nowhere with presents. What are you doing?

When you find pineapple in your pizza

when ur telling ur grandparents about ur job and they have no clue what ur talking bout but they're supportive

No train had ever touched
Thomas like this before.
His wheels felt weak.

my mental illness
my healthy coping skills
my outer self that I present to the world
@jadasyl

Use This Trick To Make Teacher Think You Are Studying While You're Eating Spaghetti

Me: Are you a wolf or a corgi?

Him: I don't know

Me: Send a pic

Hipsters or Civil War soldiers?

Recipe wanted me to beat an egg. Y'all already know what's about to go down.

When your friend keeps handing you shots

"If you are good at something never do it for free"

Me:

Increasing the temperature bit by bit during your shower to see how much your body can take

me trying to fix my rapidly deteriorating mental heath

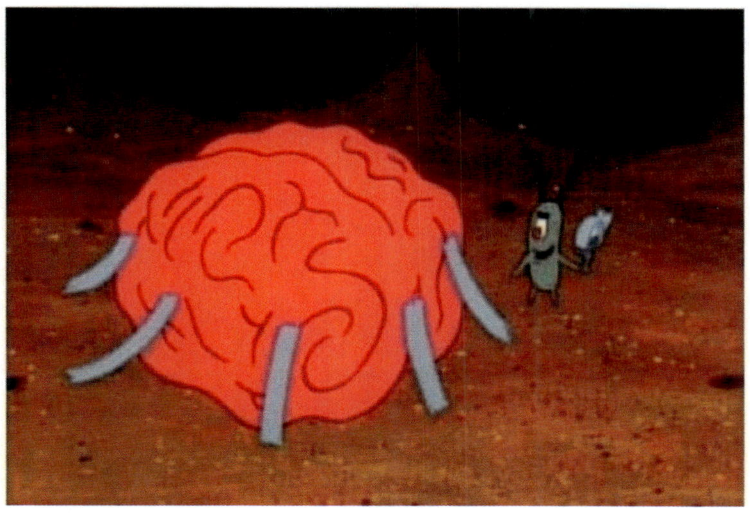

how to deal with a break up

normal people: cry, eat ice cream, watch sad movies, cry some more

steve harrington: adopt four middle-school kids and become the best single mom the hawkins high school basketball team has ever seen

throwback to last year when i made a snowman and it started to melt but refroze overnight

dark-dagger:

ah okay, that guy

When the cashier ignores your hand and places your change on the table

stuart
little
lil
stuart

Guess who's looking at memes instead of working

When you are high af and you have no idea how you got into a forest but it's kinda cool so you just accept it

YOU MATCHED WITH MIMI ON 9/16/17

if you were a vegetable, you'd be a cutecumber 😉

If I was a vegetable I'd ask you to pull the plug and end my misery

Sent

Today 8:11 PM

omg

Remember Eleven & Mike?
Here they are now. Feel old yet?

Just found a penguin skeleton in the road. Poor little fella 😢

Two actual pictures of me
showing my everyday routine

TRIED TO CATCH FOG YESTERDAY...
PLS NO...
MIST

Doorknob is short for
Doorknobert

"Does your dog bite?" Worse, he judges you

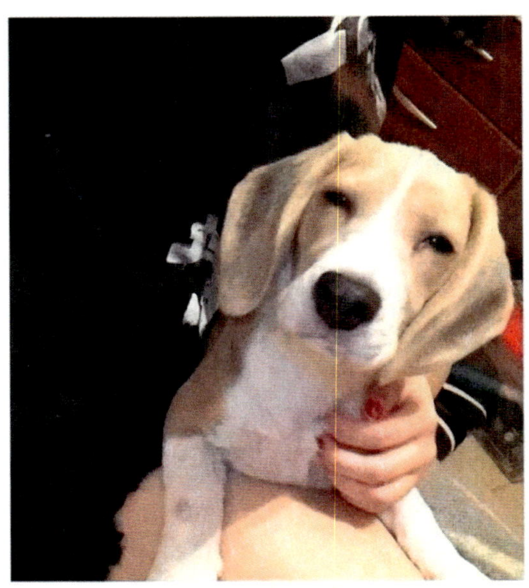

ARE YOU DOING MATH PROBLEMS FOR FUN?
YEAH. I LOVE BEING MENTALLY CHALLENGED.
WELL I'M GLAD YOU'VE COME TO TERMS WITH IT.
THANKS!

Me before christmas
vs me after christmas

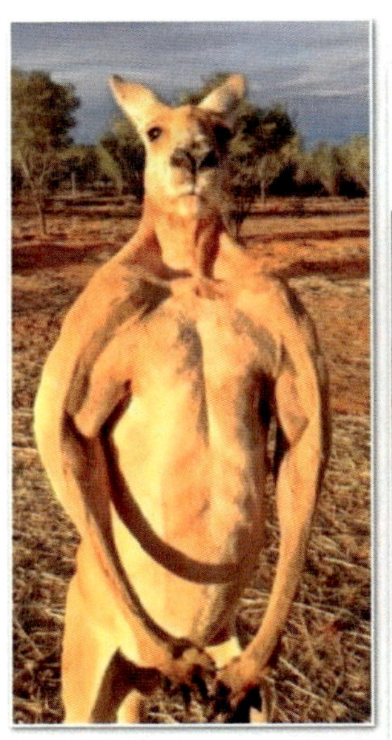

$25

$5 shipping

$30

Free shipping

my last two brain cells after I accidentally said 'love you' to the bus driver instead of 'thank you'

hate when older people say "you're too young to be tired" alright margaret you're too old to be alive but here we are

The year is 2017. Memes are now illegal, the government has taken full control of the internet, there are no more memes available, meme guards are everywhere, meme dealers whisper memes to those who are willing to pay $150 in dark alleyways, children everywhere are crying, the world has come to an end. The world is truly.....memeingless

me: *bites inside of cheek when chewing on food*

me:

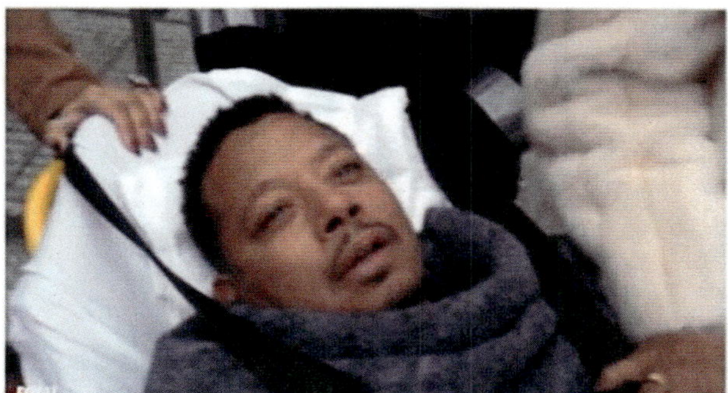

hits blunt

Bruh if you think about it, the brain named itself

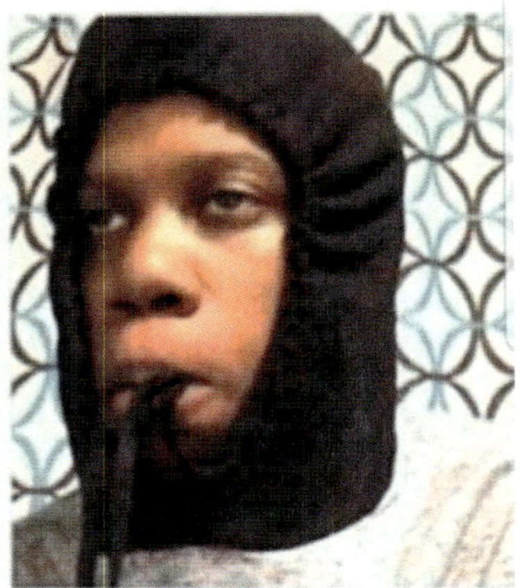

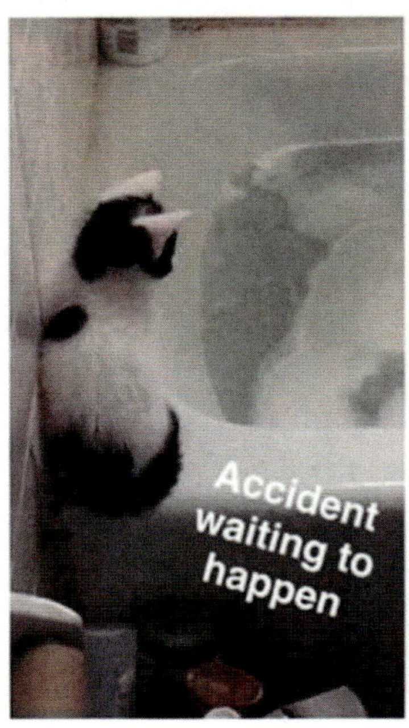

lmao they turned cars into a real thing

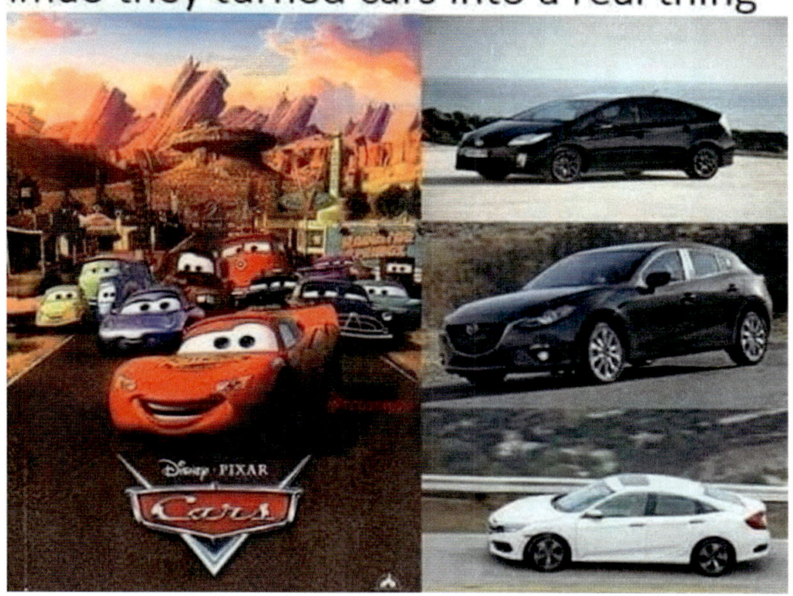

Damn how hard is it to spell Brandon?
@Starbucks

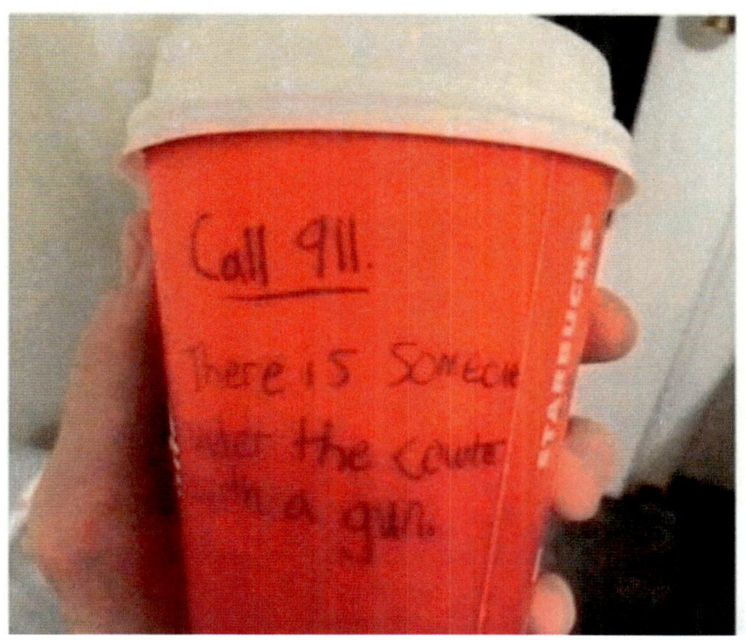

Naming Link "my dude" turns everyone you meet into a very chill bro

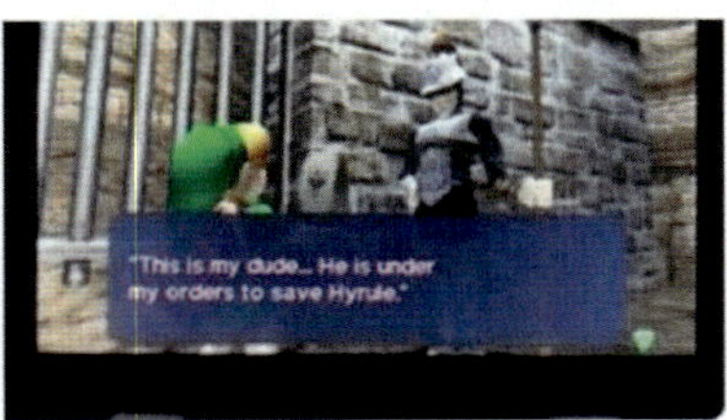

INTERNATIONAL: Bored man hacks into giant billboard so he can play Runescape while stuck in traffic

By Independent (UK)
October 6, 2016

j 13 s b f h 0 13 SHARES

When you and your friend were supposed to hang out but you both knew it wasn't going to happen

---

shakes box

I hope it's a dog

U don't know concentration until u have to carry this from the sink to the fridge

When the groupchat is in crisis but you kinda like the drama

Students drank so much alcohol at college frat party that air in house registered on breathalyser, police say

When your boss comes around so you have to pretend like you're working on something

My neighbors just added Santa hats to their Halloween decorations

what if i was cool

oh wait

i am

it's almost that time.

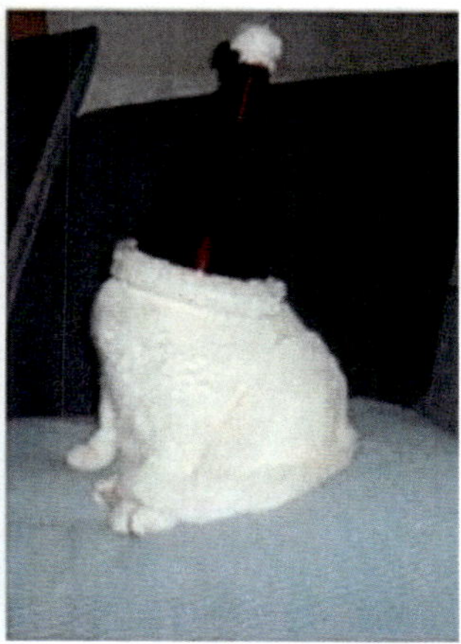

cashier: your card isn't working, do you want me to try again?

me: yes

everyone's getting into relationships and you know what im getting?

some more food brb

after eating 37 olives straight out of jar while standing in front of refrigerator at 1:34am

2:12am... going back for more olive

When your teacher asks where you see yourself in 10 years

when the check engine light comes on and you don't know shit about cars but you're an independent woman who don't need no man

So my dad waited all year to drop this certified dad joke 🤦 #Christmas 🍪

When you take your girl to mcdonalds for her birthday and she start lookin a little too far from the dollar menu

when u real sad tryin not to cry and then the moment someone asks "is everything ok?"

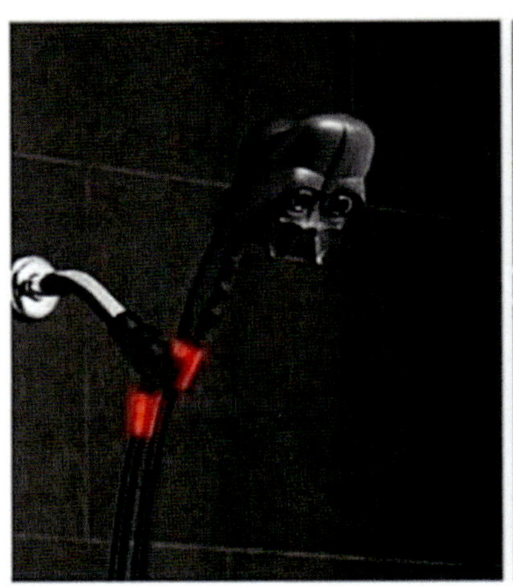

Might as well become a console since y'all tryna play me anyways

Never travel with this guy

I believe Japan doesn't
yet understand Christmas

goes college daily, nothing happens.
when you skip one day:

Stay in school

I can't imagine the things this hotel air conditioner has seen

When you asked your parents for some legos for Christmas but they get a divorce instead

Living with your parents vs. living on your own

Her.- do you have a dog or a cat?
me.- I don't know.

this scene is so sad. vader made a nice meal for everyone and han solo just starts shooting like a dickhead

A deer entered a shop. The owner decided to give him some biscuits. He left...half an hour later he came back with the squad

new years resolution: "Eat Healthy! Don't do drugs! Always look your best!"

january 1st:

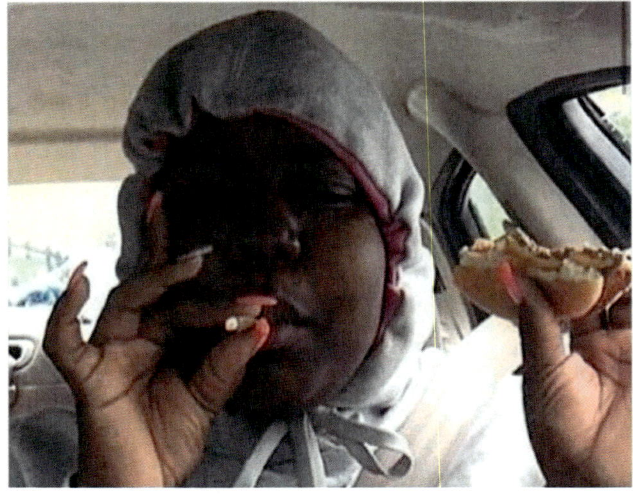

When your friend is about to do some stupid shit but you kind of want to see what happens

For only $6 a month, you can help this Ugandan find de way

HE
KNEW
DE
WEY
WHEN
NO
ONE
ELSE
DID

I prefer the real Knuckles
I said, the real Knuckles
Perfection

I can hear the "wowwwww" from here

Owen Activity @OwenActivityy

Owen Wilson staring down a paparazzi

Stress level: the part in Chicken Run where Babs knits her own noose

Teacher: use dandelion in a sentence

Jamaican: de cheetah is faster dandelion

Whole class:

DA QUEEN
DE WAY

"AFTER ALL THIS TIME?"
always
ultra thin
18

YOUR KOALAFICATIONS ARE
COMPLETELY IRRELEPHANT

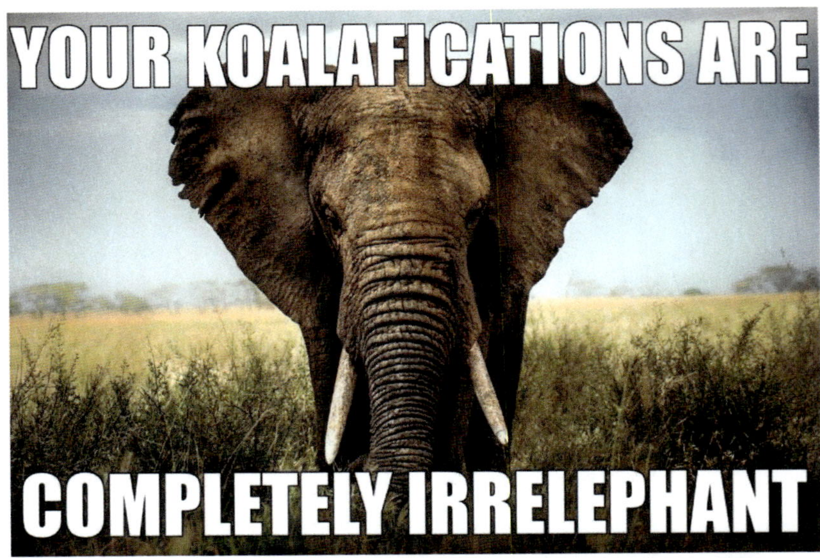

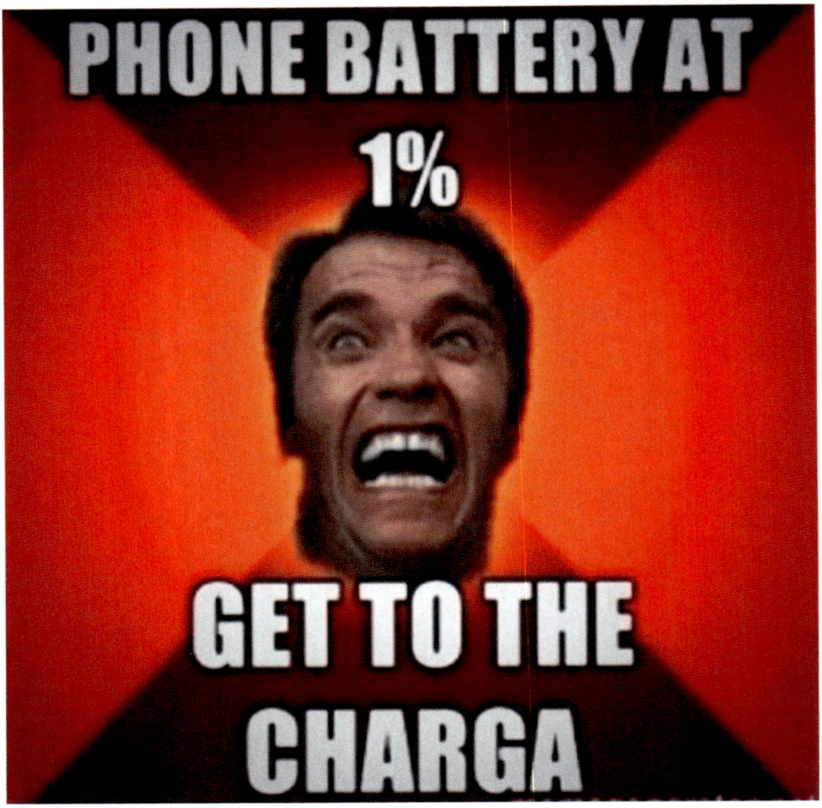
PHONE BATTERY AT
1%
GET TO THE
CHARGA

When people get mad and speed past you and y'all end up at the same red light together.

they always ask for de way...
but what if there is no way?

BUT TEACHER!!!!
HE WAS ALSO TALKING!!!!

Boys with facial hair 😍

can a crip donate blood

can a teacher give a homeless kid homework

what color are mirrors

what does water taste like

if i weigh 99 pounds and eat a pound of nachos, am i 1% nacho

Read 22:13

if sperm makes babies and is found in testicles then ball really is life

NOW THAT'S
ONE DANK MEME
YOU GOT THERE.

Animal Puns
Quack me up!

IT'S NOT A LIE
IF YOU BELIEVE IT

I'll be...
Bach.

Dwayne "The Wok" Johnson

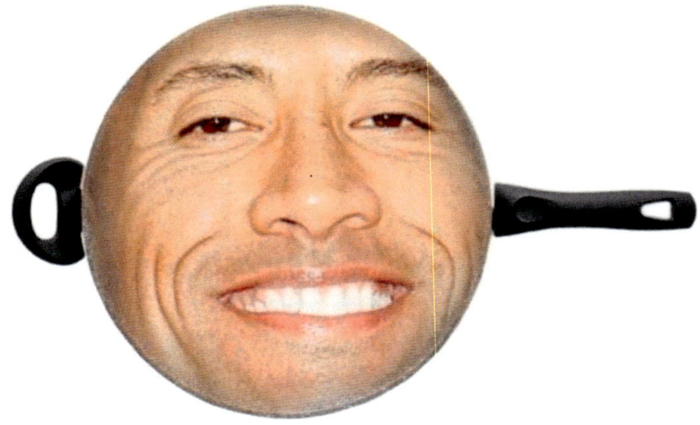

When you're sleeping and your alarm didn't ring yet but the amount of sleep you're getting is suspicious

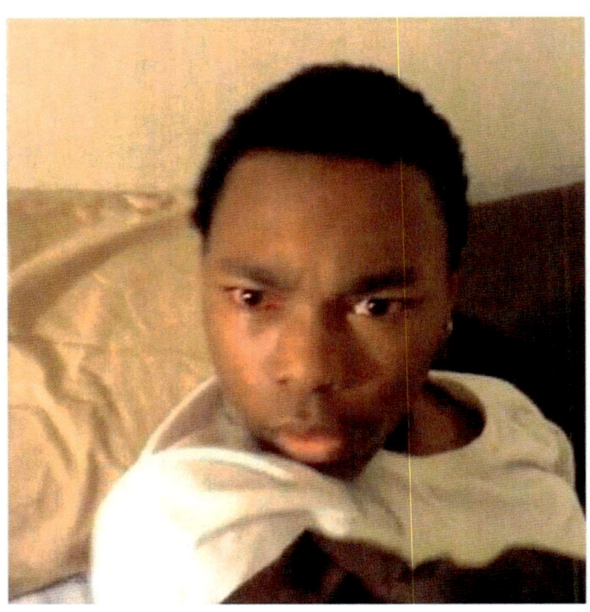

When someone ask if you know the person who knows the way

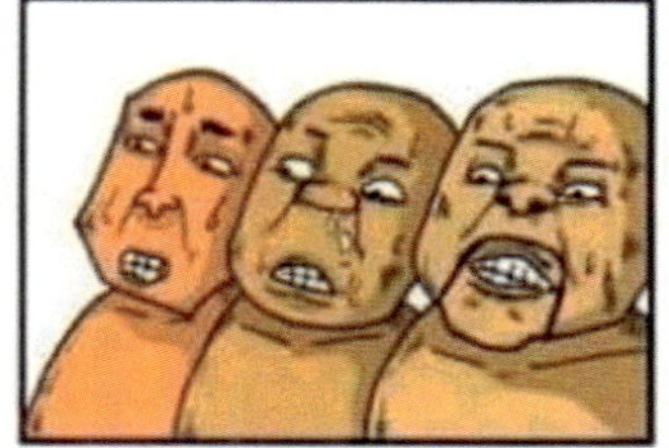

When someone says "heck" on your christian minecraft server and you let it slide but then just 10 minutes later he says "frick"

When you're taking a while to order, and hear the person behind you in line say "omg" under their breath.

When you refuse to poo on any toilet but your own and you finally make it home 💩❤️

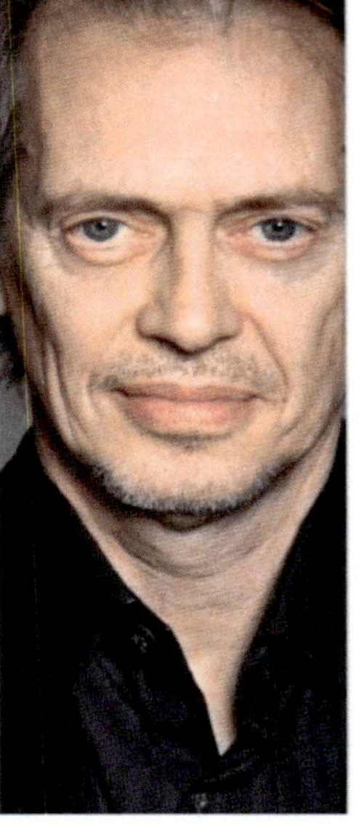

A cookie that looks like Steve Buscemi 😂😂😂

When you're about to leave work and the boss says "Before you go.."

Y'ALL GOT ANY MORE OF THEM
SPICY MEMES?

IF YOU HAVE TACOS...
I WILL FIND THEM, AND I WILL
EAT THEM.

I Have Lost de wey

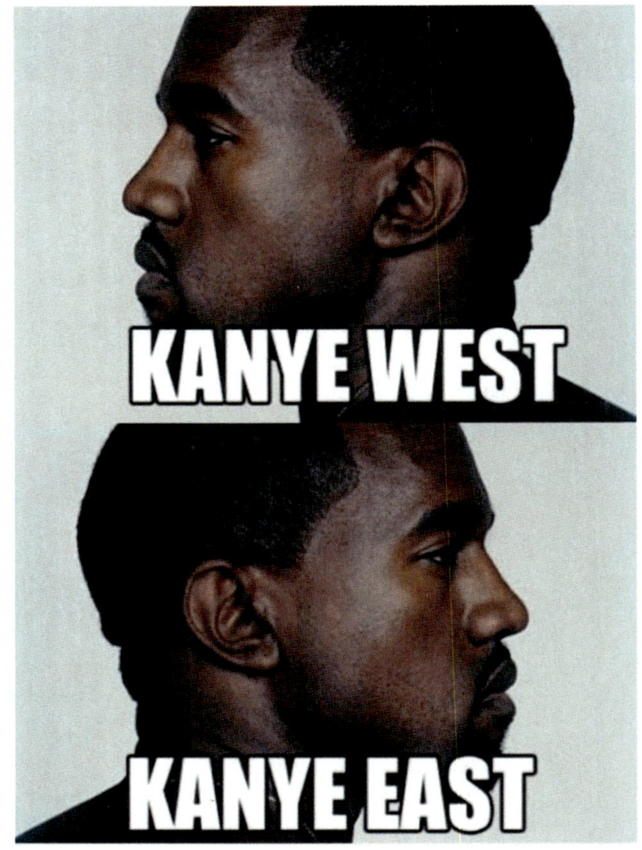
KANYE WEST
KANYE EAST

THIS FISH IS SO RAW
ITS STILL LOOKING FOR NEMO

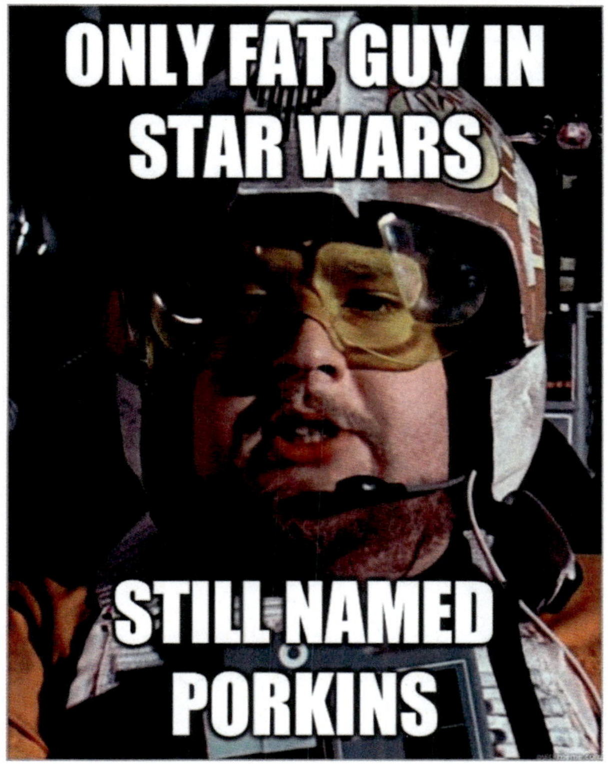
ONLY FAT GUY IN
STAR WARS
STILL NAMED
PORKINS

I'M NOT ANTI-SOCIAL,
I'M SELECTIVELY SOCIAL.
THERE'S A DIFFERENCE.

STOP MAKING ME LAUGH
YOU'LL MAKE ME PUMA PANTS

HAVE YOU SEEN THE NEW MOVIE CONSTIPATED?
IT HASN'T COME OUT YET!

TRYING NOT TO FART
WHILE SITTING NEXT TO YOUR CRUSH

BACK IN MY DAY
PEOPLE HAD BRAINS
AND WE USED
THIS TO THINK

LUKE...
I DON'T CARE

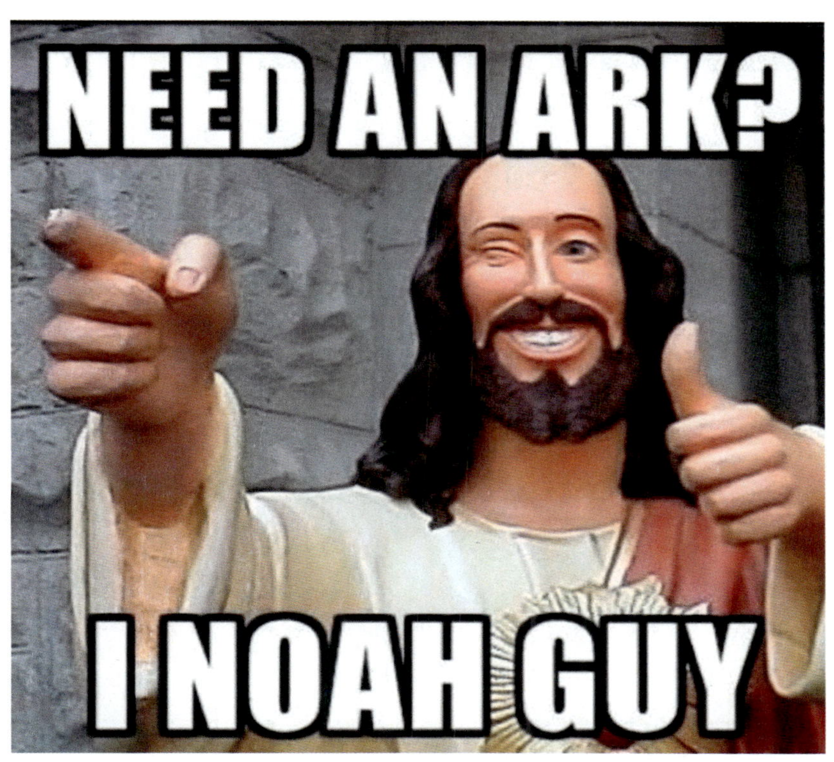
NEED AN ARK?
I NOAH GUY

I LIKE THE SOUND
YOU MAKE
WHEN YOU SHUT UP

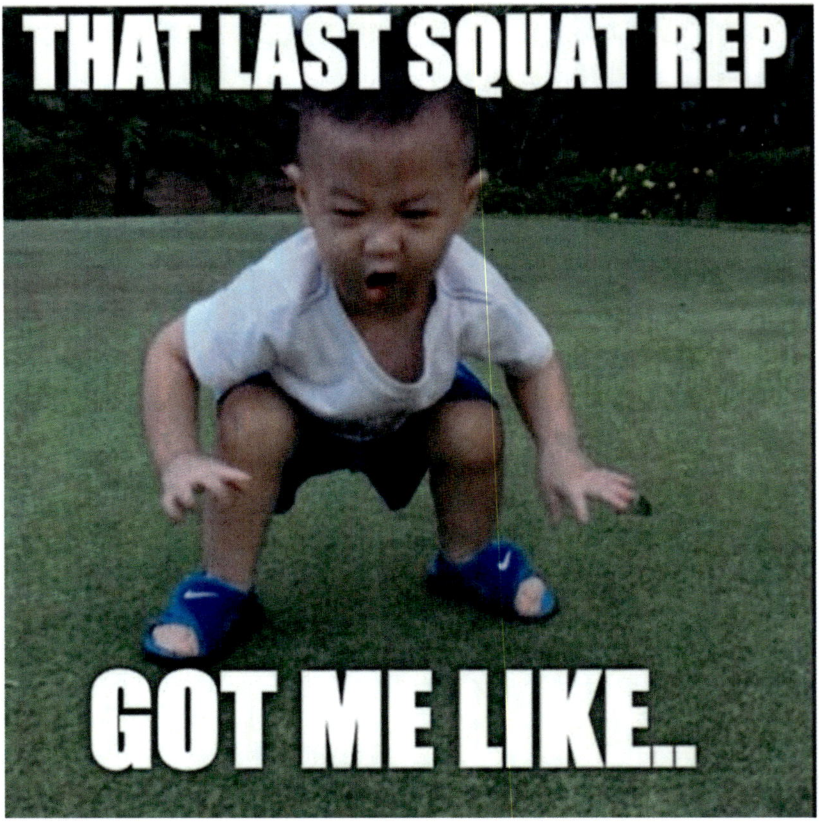
THAT LAST SQUAT REP
GOT ME LIKE..

THATS
EMUSING

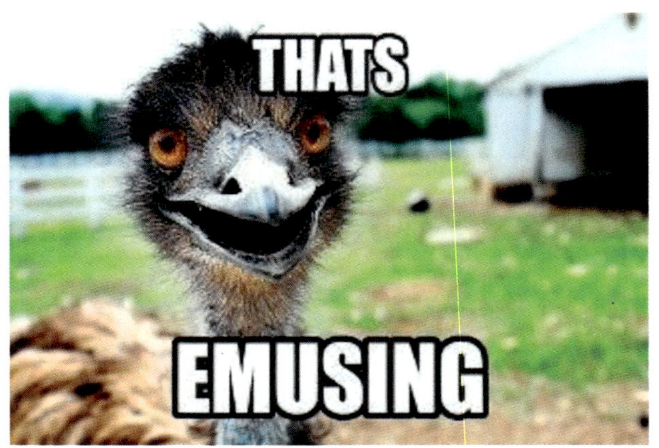

IF NICOLAS CAGE CAN STILL GET WORK
THEN YOU CAN DO ANYTHING

WHEN YOU'RE THE REASON
FOR THE COMPANY SAFETY VIDEO

When your friends are making plans without you and you gotta act like you don't care

Snapechat

I DON'T KNOW WHO YOU ARE, BUT I WILL FIND YOU AND I WILL KILL YOU.
YOU'RE RIGHT, YOU DON'T KNOW WHO THIS IS.

THATS MY DOG

MY HAPPY
FRIDAY FACE!

when the netflix asks if ur "still watching" and u see ur reflection in the black screen

runs-on-ramen:

necessary:

he needs those parts for his space ship

he's going to otter space

THAT AWKWARD MOMENT WHEN
YOU'VE ALREADY SAID "WHAT?" THREE TIMES N STILL HAVE NO IDEA WHAT THE PERSON SAID. SO YOU JUST AGREE

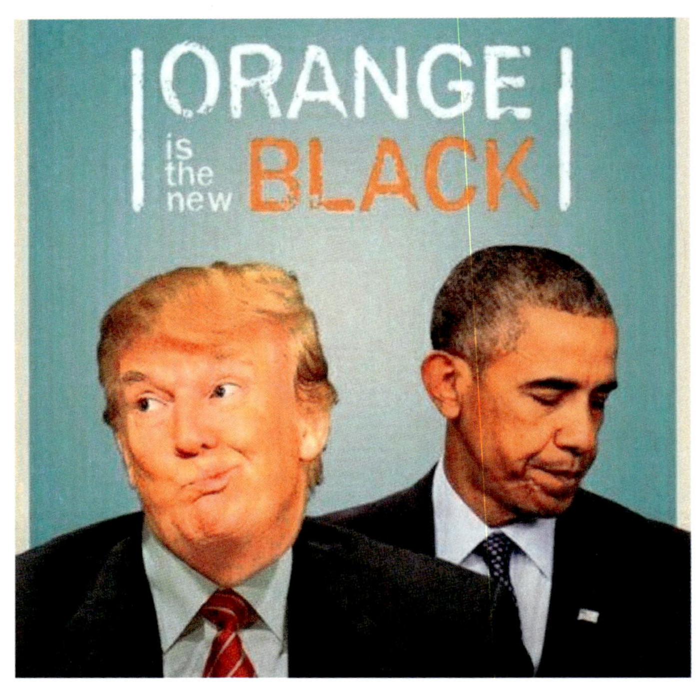
ORANGE
is the new BLACK

THAT FACE YOU MAKE
WHEN YOUR MOM MAKES
YOUR FAVOURITE FOOD

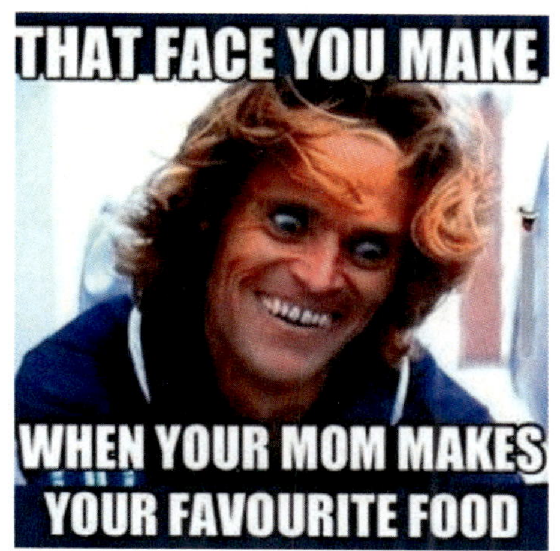

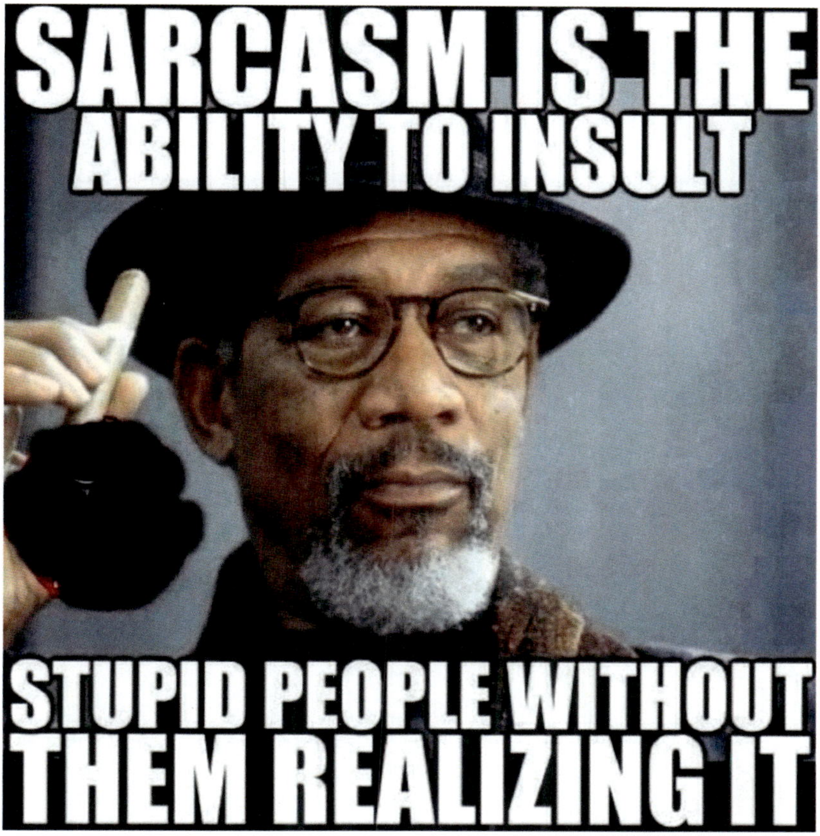
SARCASM IS THE
ABILITY TO INSULT
STUPID PEOPLE WITHOUT
THEM REALIZING IT

trying to walk when you're drunk

WHEN I FIND YOU
THE CONSEQUENCES WILL BE UNBEARABLE

EXCUSE ME SIR
DO YOU HAVE A MOMENT TO TALK ABOUT JESUS CHRIST

When your parents make a joke and you need money

Dwane "The Bop" Johnson

FREE FOOD?
COUNT ME IN!

Only in America...
do we accept weather predictions from
a rodent but deny climate change
evidence from scientists.

when you call shotgun but end up in the back

Dwayne "the Spock" Johnson

Whenever I'm in a group photo everyone else looks good and I end up looking like

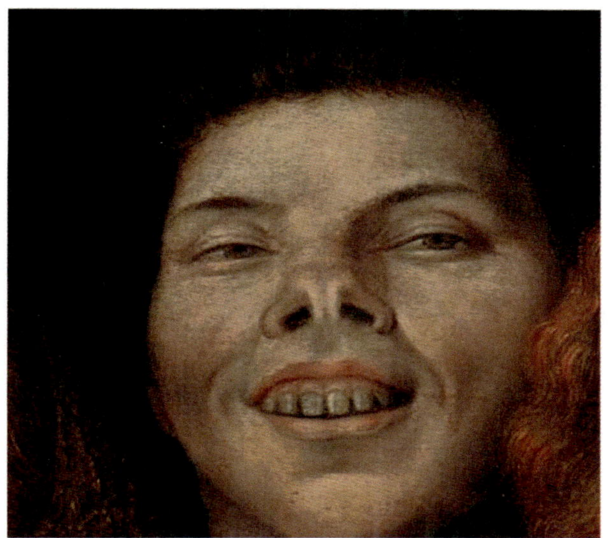

2pm, a local gas station. Drake gently runs his hand across the hood of the car as he fills his tank.

"now only one of us is empty" he thinks

I HAVE THE NECESSARY
KOALAFICATIONS

I like food and sleep
If I give you my food or text you
all night, you're special to me

THAT FACE YOU MAKE BEFORE YOU SNEEZE
I FEEL IT

I LOVE SLEEP
BECAUSE ITS LIKE A TIME MACHINE TO BREAKFAST

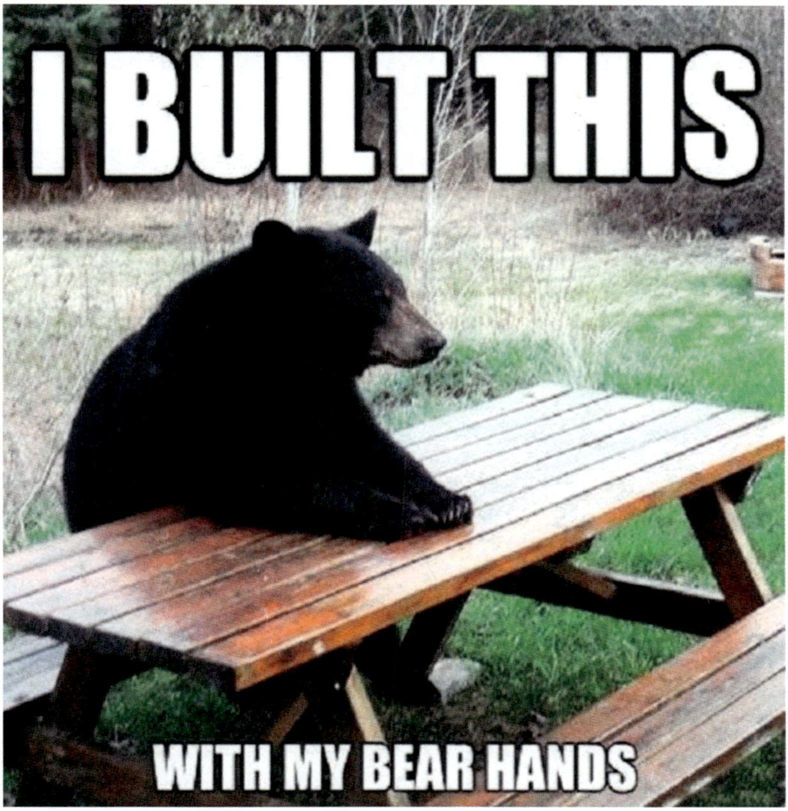
I BUILT THIS
WITH MY BEAR HANDS

In my hand
is an invisible taco
for your birthday.

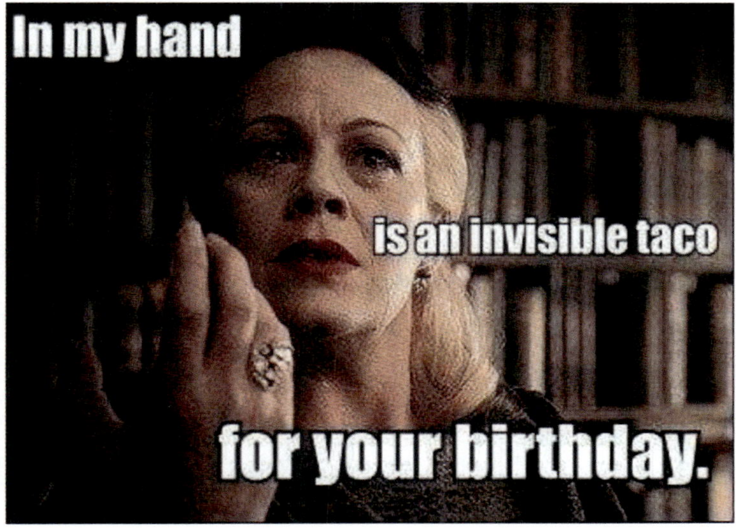

when you high in front of your parents

HEY
ARNOLD!

THAT MOMENT WHEN YOU
REALIZE
IT WASN'T A FART

i may be blind
but at least i'm not black

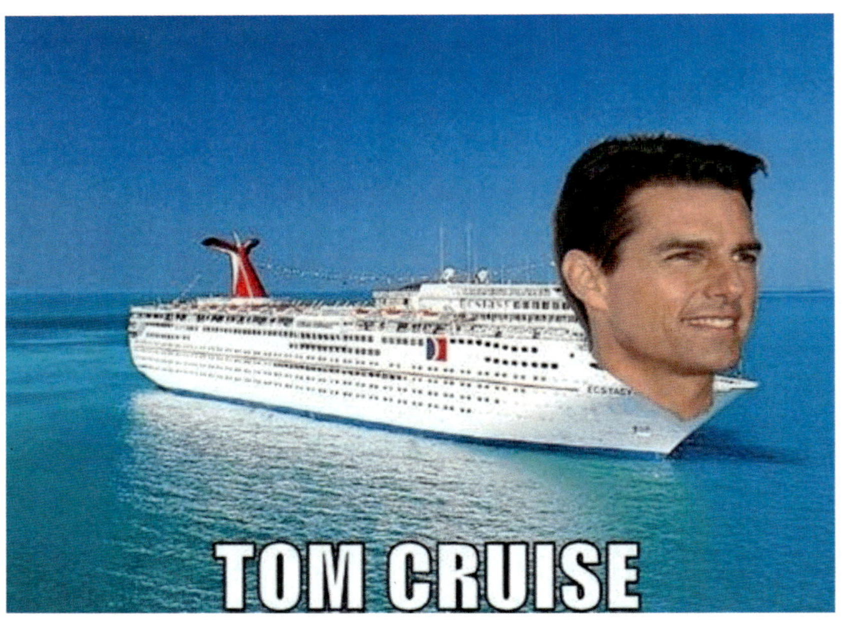
TOM CRUISE

SO I'M LOOKING FOR THIS ASIAN GUY
WHAT DOES HE LOOK LIKE?

Firefox has encountered
an unexpected problem with Windows

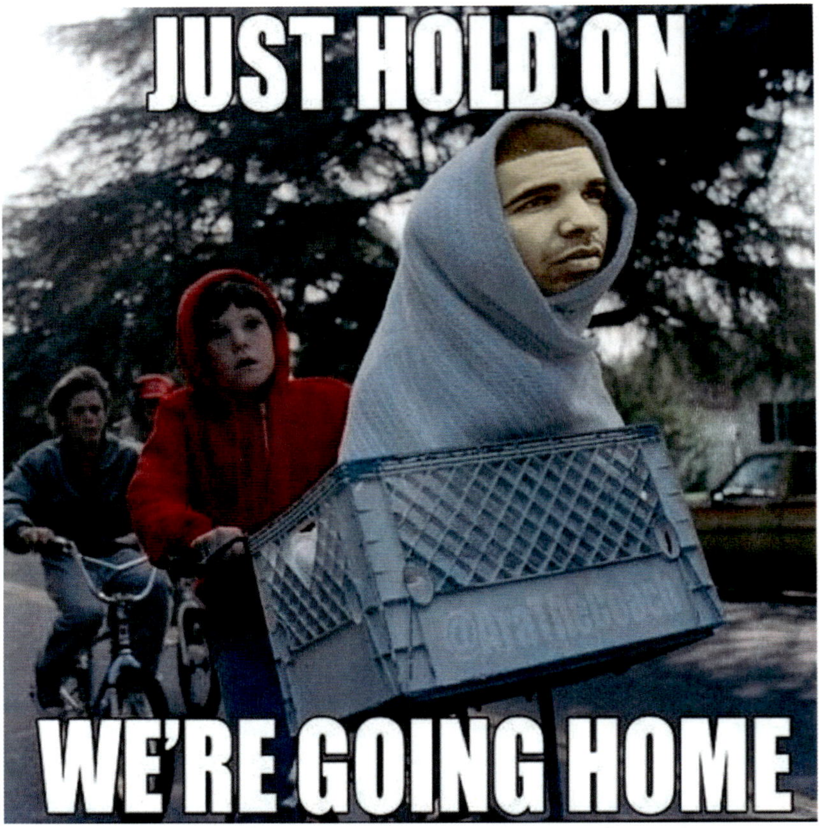

JUST HOLD ON

WE'RE GOING HOME

When your owner comes home smelling like a different dog..

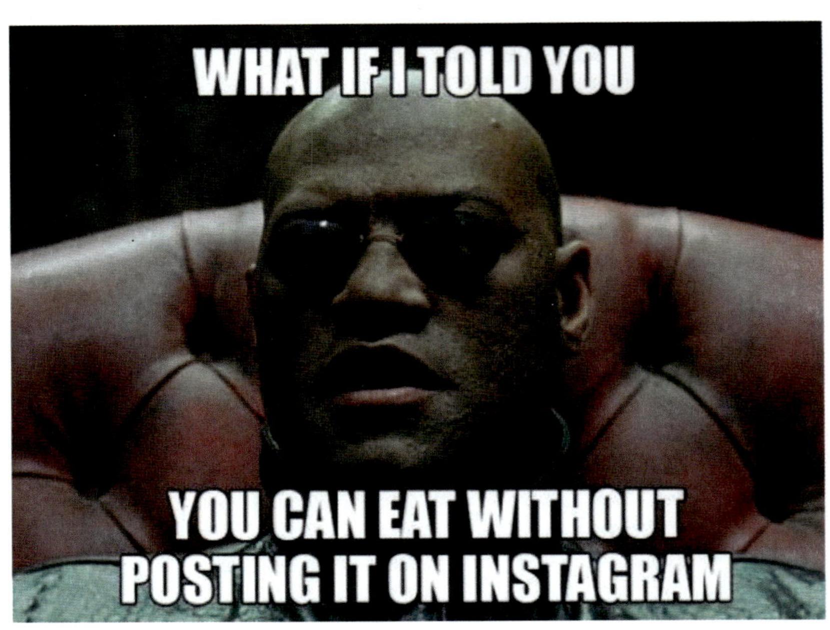
WHAT IF I TOLD YOU
YOU CAN EAT WITHOUT
POSTING IT ON INSTAGRAM

The club can't
even handle me
right now.

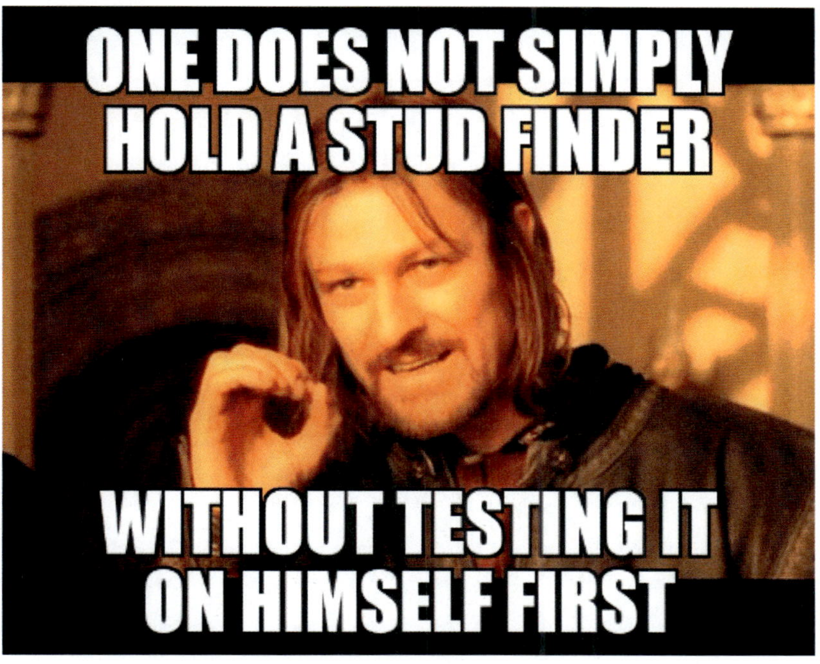

Wife rolls eyes...

WHAT ARE YOU?

AN IDIOT SANDWICH.

HEY, I JUST MET YOU AND
THIS IS CRAZY
BUT I THINK I LOVE YOU,
HAVE MY BABY.

THIS LAMB IS SO UNDERCOOKED
IT'S FOLLOWING MARY TO SCHOOL

getting online for the first time in a week like
Memes

WHEN PEOPLE SING
HAPPY BIRTHDAY TO YOU
AND YOU JUST SIT THERE LIKE...

THAT'S THE
SEALIEST THING I'VE EVER HEARD

WHEN SOMEONE RE-GIFTS
YOU A FRUIT CAKE

Snapes on a Plane

YOU'RE A UNIT OF POWER, HARRY
I'M A WATT?

YOU'RE WHITE
NO, I'M BLACK
LOL
STOP JOKING
I'M SIRIUS

when your mom gets home and the atmosphere of fun and relaxation is gone and she start yelling for no reason

MIST
IS LIKE WATER DUST

LEAVE ME ALONE!
I HAVE A LEG CRAMP!

Conclusion

Thanks again for taking the time to download this book!

You should now have a good understanding of memes , where they come from and what they are.

If you enjoyed this book, please take the time to leave me a review on Amazon. I appreciate your honest feedback, and it really helps me to continue producing high quality books.

Simply CLICK HERE to leave a review, or click on the link: (Insert link here).

Made in the USA
Las Vegas, NV
08 November 2021

33964893R00121